How to
Acquire
Properties
for just
£1

. . . .

Learn how to produce wealth from property
using the power of a simple contract

How to
Acquire
Properties
for just
£1

· · · · · · · · · · · · · · · ·

*Learn how to produce wealth from property
using the power of a simple contract*

Peter Hogan

Published by Trimore Investments

First published in 2011 by
Trimore Investments
63 The Lagger
Chalfont St Giles
Buckinghamshire
HP8 4DJ

A CIP catalogue record for this book is available from the British Library

ISBN 978–0–9570457–0–5

Lovingly created by Infinite Authors
Printed in Great Britain by Marston Book Services, Abingdon

Disclaimer

Please note that the information in this book is given as general guidance and in good faith, but does not constitute professional advice. Neither the publisher, distributor nor author can accept liability or responsibility for any loss or liability which may arise from reliance on information contained in this book.

Contents

Acknowledgements

As always, no book is written without the help, directly or indirectly, of other people, and this book is no different. My grateful thanks therefore go first to my mother, who was always my rock, and who sadly passed away in March 2011. She is very much missed.

Grateful thanks go also to my very good friend Jeanius, also known as Jean Farrall. Besides being my (not so) silent business partner, Jeanius also edited the manuscript for this book, and it is a wonderful job wot she done. She did not miss a single error.

Also to all my friends who have given me moral support and encouragement: thank you.

Introduction

Times change. No matter what business you are in, business methods change. The economy changes, we have times of boom, times of recession, and no one business model can cope with everything.

There have been massive changes over the last few years in the property market. The crash was inevitable: when the market is

When the market is super-heated that is the time to get out, not in

such that if you don't make a firm offer on a property during the viewing you lose out, when prices are increasing by up to £40,000 *per week*, (yes, I've seen it), when you can get £10,000 cash-back when buying a property the market is super-heated. That's the time to get out, not in. Or at least, not use your capital to get in.

Creative investors, however, will always find a way to succeed, to make money. Post crash we saw the rise of 25% or more BMV (below market value) sales, 'No Money Down', etc. but even these have become nearly impossible now. More recently 'lease options' has become the buzz phrase, and for very good reason. Many homeowners have suffered greatly in the last few years and are now struggling to pay their mortgages; repossessions are at their highest for many years, are forecast to go even higher as interest rates rise and will rise still more steeply if the widely predicted double-dip recession hits.

Many of the hardest-hit homeowners bought at, or near to, the top of the market, in the years from 2005 to 2008, sometimes with 110% LTV (loan-to-value) mortgages and often with loans to refurbish the property as well. A lack of equity, and sometimes even negative equity, means they cannot reduce the price of their home to a point where it will sell without incurring a loss, leaving them with no alternative but to hand the keys back to the bank or have their home repossessed, and possibly face bancruptcy as well.

Many homeowners have struggled greatly in the past few years

A canny investor can use this situation to his or her advantage. A lease option contract, properly used, can mean business for the investor, a solution for the vendor, and even a solution for the banks, in that they don't have to repossess another property! It's a winning situation all round.

So immerse yourself in lease options and watch your portfolio grow rapidly, all with very little capital investment.

1

What a lease option is, and what it isn't

A lease option is simply a specific type of contract. They have been used for many years in the USA and Australia, and are now finding popularity in the UK as lending restrictions and criteria make obtaining a mortgage extremely difficult.

What is a lease option?

A lease option is a combination of two main contracts, a lease, and an option to buy. You negotiate a term for the lease – anything from a few months up to twenty years, although the average at the moment is between seven and ten years to give the market time to recover – and agree to lease the property from the vendor for up to that time. You also agree a future purchase price for the property, and can then purchase the property for the agreed **A lease option is simply a specific type of contract** price any time within the option period if you so desire. The point is, you have the *option* to buy: you don't have to if you don't want to, but if you do, the seller cannot refuse to sell.

Often, our 'vendors' will be homeowners who, for one reason or another, have fallen into financial hardship; maybe they've lost their job or maybe they simply can't manage their finances and have built up too much debt. Increasingly these days they are divorcing, and need to sell their home quickly. Maybe they are moving for work, or just to be nearer to family. Regardless, our vendors are are usually past the 'motivated seller' stage and are often 'distressed sellers'. This means they are vulnerable, desperate, stressed and anxious to find a very quick solution to their problem. Unscrupulous investors may see this as an opportunity to extract the very maximum from the vendors: to screw them for every single penny they can.

If you don't want to buy, you don't have to

I warn you against using this tactic however; it may well be your undoing. Let us look at it from the legal point of view. A contract, properly drawn up, should be watertight legally. Many contracts aren't, however, and attempting to use a contract downloaded from the internet – usually from America – and adapting it for your own use is asking for trouble. 'Off-the-shelf' contracts can cause problems down the line as well. Much better to spend a little time and money and get it right from the start. But even assuming your contract *is* watertight, it can still be contested in court on the grounds of unfairness. 'Fairness' rules in law – judges are directed to keep in mind, 'Is it fair and reasonable', when they look at cases. The courts can, and do, overturn contracts because of unreasonable terms contained within.

Let me give an example. You have a vendor who needs to sell his house very quickly because he has lost his job and is struggling to meet his mortgage liabilities. The house is worth £100,000, and his outstanding mortgage is £90,000. He has £10,000 equity, but the house has been on the market for six months already, and he has had no offers. He cannot wait any longer.

You meet with him and agree a lease option deal whereby you will take over his mortgage payments and buy his house within seven years for £90,000. You estimate the house will be worth £150,000 at that time, and you rub your hands with glee at the thought of a £60,000 payday. However, when you come to purchase the property the vendor is very upset to see the current value, and contests the contract in court. Any judge looking at those figures will almost certainly come to the conclusion that the contract is unfair, and find for the claimant. You lose big time.

The courts can, and do, overturn contracts

The terms I would choose for this property are £100,000 purchase price (today's value) plus a percentage – usually between 10% and 20%, depending on the circumstances, but in this case 20% – of the uplift in value on a RICS valuation. So at purchase the vendor would receive £100,000 plus 20% of £50,000, i.e. £10,000. In total he would walk away with £110,000.

This is good for a number of reasons, the first being that it is easier to sell the concept in the first place. The vendor is always going to feel very happy with the deal and is unlikely to contest the contract and, if he does, he is very unlikely to win, as you have obviously not been unfair or unreasonable in your terms. He is highly likely to recommend you to other people he knows who fall into similar circumstances, so you do more business. Finally of course, you sleep easier knowing that you are an honest and ethical businessperson, don't you? A lease option, indeed, any deal, should be a win–win situation. Don't underestimate the power of doing good and helping people. You definitely do not want people thinking bad things about you or wishing bad things upon you. You have heard the expression 'what goes around comes around'. Believe me, it is true. You do the dirty on people in this life and life has a way of repaying you in spades. Keep it clean and keep it honest. You'll be far more successful.

2

The difference between a lease option and a normal sale

Normal sales

Normal property sales follow a predictable pattern. To begin with you see a property you like and make an appointment with the estate agent to view it (hoping he's not a spotty youth who doesn't know what he's doing).

Next you decide you want to buy it and make an offer. The agent goes away and, hopefully, puts forward your offer. The

Normal property sales follow a predictable pattern

agent then comes back to you and (usually) says the offer isn't high enough – you need to offer more. You do so, and the agent goes away. When you next meet he says that, unfortunately, someone else has offered a higher price, and you will need to increase your offer. You do so, and the agent goes away.

At this point you start to get the feeling that perhaps, just perhaps, the agent is not being completely honest with you. But what can you do?

Eventually you make an offer that the seller – or the agent – considers reasonable, and a deal is struck. You give the agent a cheque for 10% as a deposit.

You now need to talk to a mortgage advisor, and, frequently, use the one the estate agent suggests, not knowing how good he is, or even whether he is independent or tied. You apply for a DIP, (decision in principle) and spend a considerable amount of time providing proof of income, proof of deposit, proof of residency etc. Eventually you receive your DIP.

The mortgage company now appoints a RICS surveyor to survey the property to make sure it is mortgageable and to establish its value. This is where you start to pray. Whether you know it or not, it is the surveyor who can make or break any sale. Whatever the surveyor says the value is, that is what it is. It is totally irrelevant what you, the vendor or the agent think the value is, and if the surveyor comes back with a valuation different from the agreed price, you have a problem: either you adapt, or the deal may break down.

It is the surveyor who can make or break any sale

You will probably find that the vendor needs to buy another property to move into, and cannot complete on this one until a new one is found and bought; this is the classic 'chain', which can include many vendors/buyers. Chains very often break down for any number of reasons, leaving everyone else to start again

Eventually, with luck, and some months down the line, contracts are exchanged and you can begin either finding a removal company, or finding tenants if you are letting the property.

Add up the costs involved so far – deposit, mortgage broker fee, surveyor fee, mortgage arrangement fee – and you'll soon see that it's a considerable amount!

With luck completion takes place within a few weeks and you now own the property. Oops! No you don't; the mortgage company owns it – you're buying it off them for a monthly payment. Well, at least you have control of the property, and all the stress, effort and expense was worth it, wasn't it?

Maybe, maybe not.

Lease options

Let us now look at how a lease option works. The Smith family (Mr and Mrs Smith and their two children) are in trouble. Mr Smith has been made redundant and has little prospect of finding employment. The family's finances are in a critical situation. The problem is that they have very little equity in their property, **Chains very often break down** and cannot reduce the price to a point where it will sell. They have had the house on the market for six months with a local estate agent and have not even had a viewing yet. They are desperate.

You arrange to meet with them both at their home. You agree

a deal whereby you will take over the property, and will pay the Smiths' mortgage for the for a period of seven years. You will also make sure the council tax is paid and the property fully maintained. At any time within the seven years you can buy the property if you wish at a price you agree today, regardless of what the property may be worth. You have the *right* to buy the property, but not the *obligation*; you don't have to buy it if you don't want to, but if you do want to, the Smiths cannot refuse.

You have the contracts drawn up, and all parties sign. You now have control of the property just as if you had bought it, but without the time and expense of a traditional sale. You can rent out the property, and the difference between the mortgage and the rent is your profit, plus you can look forward to a considerable profit at the end.

I have completed lease option deals in as little as three days with little or no expense.

Which method would you choose?

3

Why now is the right time

Markets change, particularly the housing market. There is a regular cycle of boom and bust. Periods of sustained and rapid growth result in a super-heated situation where prices are unstable. When you know that if you don't make an offer at the time of viewing that you will lose the property, when prices increase daily by thousands of pounds, when banks and mortgage companies are throwing money at you, you know it cannot **There's a regular cycle of boom and bust** last. A crash is inevitable, followed by a period of lacklustre performance (or even none at all) before slowly confidence in the economy starts to return, and prices gradually begin to creep upwards, gaining momentum increasingly until again, there occurs a crash and a time of reconsolidation.

At the time of writing (summer 2011) we are certainly in the doldrums. The huge US sub-prime market (most of which had been sold worldwide) was unsustainable, and the inevitable crash followed swiftly on the heels of the demise of Lehman Brothers.

The ramifications of unethical and irresponsible lending by the banks shook the financial foundations of the American and British economies.

Banks lost huge amounts of money, and new, very stringent lending criteria were put in place, making it next to impossible to secure a mortgage unless you could show you didn't need one!

At some point borrowed money, and the debt, need to be paid off

With belt-tightening across the country, the inevitable job-losses saw many people – most of whom had bought in the middle of the preceding decade at the height of the boom – unable to meet their mortgage liabilities, and the devaluation in property prices meant they just could not sell, leaving the banks with little option but to repossess.

Quantitative easing (QE) and QE2, where the government printed money and pumped it into the economy, along with interest rates at historical lows of just half a percent were intended to kick-start the economy. Millions of pounds were given to the banks with the idea that they would start to lend again and help the economic recovery. It didn't happen. The banks held on to the money and the recovery faltered, if indeed it ever started.

So where do we go from here? Property prices are low, and it would seem to be the ideal time for the investor to jump in and start buying property, right?

Well, maybe. And maybe not.

Over the last past year (2011) the banks seem to have relaxed somewhat. New mortgage products have appeared, although borrowing is still notoriously difficult. Gone are the days of the 95% (or even 100% and more) mortgage though, which means that the more prudent investor is less likely to be exposed to changes in the mortgage rate. On the other hand, a larger deposit requirement means a greater investment of one's own capital, and therefore a greater exposure to economic fluctuation.

This is not a problem though, if the economy recovers over the next couple of years, as many hope and believe it will. But is the economy en route to a recovery?

Well, maybe. And maybe not.

We in the UK are tied too closely to the USA not to be affected by their problems, and they have just lost their triple-A rating, something inconceivable even a few months ago. The once mighty dollar – the world's key currency – is looking decidedly fragile. America has had a negative trade surplus for decades, and it was only the strength of the dollar that kept the economy afloat. What now? We all know that borrowing money to pay debts is only a short-term solution, and America has just raised its maximum borrowing limit. At some point that borrowed money, and the debts, need to be repaid. It's difficult to see how America will manage that with its massive trade deficit. Whilst its exports are so far below its imports, America isn't earning enough money to pay its debts.

China, on the other hand, has a *massive* trade surplus. China is cash-rich, and has bought billions of dollars worth of American bonds. So much, in fact, that China now has leverage over the USA to the point where it has recently seen fit to comment on America's fiscal housekeeping (or lack of it). This is undoubtedly of great concern to America.

But what about the UK? The pound is strong, we still have our triple-A rating, the world still sees the UK as a safe haven for investment, so everything should turn out OK, shouldn't it?

Well, maybe. And maybe not.

The lack of lending by the banks means that many British businesses have been unable to invest in their future, leaving them unable to be competitive when the economy does recover. The strong pound makes exports expensive, and businesses and the economy suffer.

The Bank of England has kept the bank base rate low at just half a percent in an effort to stimulate the economy, but the banks have not passed on those rates in the form of lower mortgage rates. The cost of living is also rising at a far greater rate then many predicted. The usual method of controlling a high cost of living is to raise the bank rate, but the Bank of England continues to hold the rate at an artificially low level.

There are predictions that it could stay low for another couple of years or so. Eventually, though, it is going to have to go up, and it might just 'snap' up to a high level over a short period of time to make up for the years when it was too low. You can bet the banks will raise their mortgage rates as well.

That could well put may buy-to-let (BTL) investors in negative yield, and many more private homeowners will not be able to manage the extra strain on their finances. Higher interest rates mean even less borrowing. Many businesses that are struggling now will be unable to service their debt, with more job losses inevitable, so we may well have the scenario where we have a country whose export businesses are unable to compete in the world market, severely affecting our trade balance.

Many British businesses have been unable to invest in their future

Another recession – the much talked about 'double dip' – starts to seem very likely. This time, however, things could be far, far worse.

Quantitative easing did not end the recession first time around. It won't this time either, because there just isn't enough money to pump into the economy. Bringing the bank base rate down won't work, either. We'll be too far gone for that to be effective.

The current problems for the property market would intensify enormously. Sales would drop to an even lower level. Repossessions would increase. There would be a huge pool of unsellable properties. A black outlook indeed. In fact, many economists are predicting a major property crash and are advising investors to get out now while (and if) they can.

So should we heed this advice? Should we be consolidating our assets, selling our less profitable properties, buying gold and waiting until things improve before investing in property again?

Well, yes. And no.

Great Britain's property market is unique in that the strict controls on building on green zones mean that there simply are not enough houses to supply demand, and demand has risen astronomically over the last ten years.

Rental demand is at its highest, with insufficient homes available to satisfy that demand. Supply and demand dictates that renting out properties is a very good business to be in. The problem is that the economy means that we cannot buy enough properties to take advantage of the situation, and anyway, would we really want to invest our capital right now?

renting out properties is a very good business to be in

The answer to the conundrum is, of course, lease options.

The present and continuing economic situation means a huge number of properties becoming available that are unsellable. Controlling a property with a lease option means that you can take advantage of the high rental demand without exposing your capital to risk. You can structure the option over a long enough period to be pretty sure of making a healthy profit at the back end, too.

So, being able to capitalize on the recession with little or even zero exposure and risk whilst making increasingly higher profits, is obviously a smart way to invest.

4

Sourcing leads

The most popular part of my courses and seminars is always the 'how to' bit; how to negotiate, how to stack a deal, how to find finance and, of course, how to source leads. This doesn't surprise me. After all, if you don't know how to find a deal you won't get very far in the property business, and it's always this part that most people, and new investors in particular, have the most trouble mastering.

There are a number of ways of marketing your business, and that is what you are doing after all: making people aware of what you do. Leaflets, direct mail, newspaper adverts, sandwich boards, sign-written vehicles and estate agents are all methods used to attract customers.

1. Leaflets

I like leaflets. At the end of January 1997 I started a hardwood flooring business in London and created all my leads from leaflets. I learned very quickly how important copy writing is, what works, and what doesn't. I started by putting out 10,000 leaflets per month, and work flooded in. By the end of the year – eleven months of trading – I had turned over £465,000. In year two I increased leaflet distribution to 50,000 per month and my turnover was £1,000,000. In year three I turned over £1,200,000. My 'area' was London and within the M25.

The beauty of leaflets is that you can target your vendors precisely. In fact, trying to kill two or even three birds with one stone by attempting to target too large a spread of vendors – BMV, lease options, commercial, etc. – just doesn't work. Decide who your target is and write the leaflet directly for him or her.

Despite what many people would have you believe, size *is* important, at least where leaflets are concerned. My flooring company leaflets were A4 glossy, two colour, single sided and folded. They worked a treat, but were expensive, even more so as I put them out as a single drop (that is when your leaflet is the only one put through the door, instead of a multi-drop, where the delivery is shared with maybe four or five other leaflets).

The beauty of leaflets is that you can target your vendors precisely

As cost is usually an issue, I would suggest beginning with a single-sided A5 leaflet on lightweight paper (which could be coloured, e.g. yellow) and sending it out as part of a multi-drop.

Before you have your leaflets printed, spend some time selecting your distributor. Distributors generally have lots of local knowledge and their expertise can save you a fortune in wasted drops. Tell them exactly the type of homeowner you want to target and they should be able to tell you areas that will be more productive. All distributors seem to have deals going with printers, and you will generally save a lot of money by using their suggested printer rather than going to one independently.

The more leaflets you have printed, the lower the unit cost will be; an economy of scale. You can have 50,000 printed for not much more than the cost of 10,000. However, if you haven't 'proved' your leaflet – established its effectiveness – you may decide to change

Your leaflet is a 10 second sales pitch

the copy before you have used all 50,000, and find you have wasted your money on unused leaflets.

Professional copywriters are expensive, and you can do a good a job yourself with a little thought. The internet has made this kind of research easy. Just Google 'copywriting' and fifty squillion pages will come up in half a nanosecond.

The principles of writing a leaflet are common sense really. Think about what you do when mail-shots come through your letterbox. Generally, you bin the lot, unless one of them catches your eye. If one does, you give it a maximum of about three seconds to establish if it is of genuine interest to you. That is what your target vendors will do, so you have to try to catch their attention very quickly.

You could do this with coloured paper, but be aware that many colours just don't work: type does not show up well on green, purple, red or blue, for example. Yellow is perhaps the best colour to choose, as it will show both black and red copy well. Your leaflet is really a ten-second sales pitch and should follow a basic sales structure, that is:

- Identify the problem;

- Have the target acknowledge it;

- Provide an answer or solution;

- Make it easy for them to follow through, i.e. to contact you.

Putting their mind at ease about their situation will improve results.

At the top of the leaflet the first line has just one purpose: to get readers to read line two. That line, therefore, is the 'catcher'. It is the one that has to capture the reader's interest, so it should be big, eye-catching and relevant. Now you need to put yourself in your target's shoes again. What problems are they facing, and therefore what problems will you be attempting to solve for them?

Nine times out of ten they will be an owner who needs to sell, but can't. They may have lost their job or be divorcing, but usually there will be underlying financial problems, possibly even repossession and bankruptcy looming. Their financial problems will be constantly on their mind, causing a lot of stress. It makes sense therefore that the top line, in large red font, could read;

MONEY TROUBLES???

That line jumps off the page. Anyone reading that question will answer it in their mind; 'Yes, that's me' or 'No'. If they answer 'yes', they will continue reading the leaflet, as the information is pertinent to their problem and could help them. Now, they could have all sorts of money troubles; credit card debts for example, which, if they are living in rented accommodation is not an area in which we are interested. We need to narrow down the financially-troubled targets to those who own their home but are struggling with the mortgage, so line two could read;

CAN'T PAY THE MORTGAGE???

Now those with no mortgage – the renters – will lose interest and those with a mortgage will again say 'Yes, that's me'. At this point it is important that you are not perceived to be attaching blame to the target; most people trying to cope with this type of stress will often put the blame on others rather than themselves, and may be sensitive to the thought that other people see them as being at fault, so now we could say:

IF YOU'RE IN FINANCIAL DIFFICULTY
THE BANKS CAN BE LESS THAN HELPFUL
THEY MAY EVEN BE TALKING REPOSSESSION

Here we make the banks the baddie; it's really *their* fault that the vendor is in financial trouble; the banks wouldn't help. Now, though, we come to the rescue:

DON'T WORRY

After identifying their problem, bringing it out into the open and making them worry, we now tell them not to, and it's a command. There has to be a reason for them not to worry though, a potential solution to their problem, so we give it to them.

EVEN IF YOU ARE IN NEGATIVE EQUITY AND CANNOT SELL WE MAY STILL BE ABLE TO

HELP YOU

The words 'help you' are larger for a reason; they jump off the page, and will stick in the reader's mind because, as they read it, they place greater emphasis on the words, helping to cement them in their mind. Now we need to tell them how to get the help we have promised:

DON'T LEAVE IT ANY LONGER. CALL NOW FOR A CHAT TO SEE HOW WE CAN HELP

Again, these are commands. People respond to commands. We don't want them to call tomorrow; they will have forgotten by then. We want them to call *now*.

The words 'we can help' are on a separate line for a reason;

they stand out and can be seen in isolation from the rest of the sentence, reinforcing our 'help' message. Now we need the contact details:-

MY NAME IS JOHN AND MY NUMBER IS
12345 345 567

Up to this point we have been anonymous but now we need to become personal, to be their friend. Friends call each other by their first name, so we use one. 'John', in this case, but it could be any appropriate name. Use a number that will be answered by you, and don't use a mobile number. You can use your home number and switch it to your mobile whilst you are out, or even get an 0800 number to use. 0800 numbers can also be switched to your mobile permanently.

Put all the elements of the leaflet together and you have the sample shown on the next page. This is a 'proven' leaflet; I know it works because I and many of my course attendees use it. You can use it as is, or adapt it to your own particular requirements.

2. Direct mail

Direct mail can be a very effective way of targeting people. Potential properties, those which have been on the market for a long time and obviously are not selling, can be identified by a variety methods; drive-past, newspaper ads, internet and a letter sent directly to the address. The effectiveness of the letter can be very much increased by using the homeowner's name. This

MONEY TROUBLES???

CAN'T PAY THE MORTGAGE???

IF YOU'RE IN FINANCIAL DIFFICULTY
THE BANKS CAN BE LESS THAN HELPFUL

THEY MAY EVEN BE TALKING REPOSSESSION

DON'T WORRY

EVEN IF YOU ARE IN NEGATIVE
EQUITY AND CANNOT SELL WE
MAY STILL BE ABLE TO

HELP YOU

DON'T LEAVE IT ANY LONGER
CALL NOW FOR A CHAT TO SEE HOW
WE CAN HELP

MY NAME IS JOHN
AND MY NUMBER IS
12345 345 567

can be established by asking neighbours, a census search or by a land registry search, although the latter will cost you £4. A very important point is to hand write the letter. A handwritten envelope addressed to a person by name is almost guaranteed to be opened, and a personalized handwritten letter within will certainly elicit more response than a printed 'Dear Homeowner' type of letter.

A sample letter could be as follows:

Dear Mr and Mrs Smith,

I hope you don't mind my writing this letter, but I have noticed that your home has been up for sale for a long time and it seems that you haven't yet been able to find a buyer.

Times are difficult, I know, and it looks like things might even get worse if there is another recession, as many people are predicting. However, I am interested in your house and I wonder if we could have a chat to see if there is anything we can do.

My name is John Jones and my number is 12345 345 456. Please feel free to call me anytime.

Yours sincerely,

John Jones.

PS I am able to move quickly if that will help as there is no chain involved on my side.

A 'PS' is very effective at getting a point across, and you will often see them used in marketing. In fact you will often see 'PPS' , 'PPPS' and even 'PPPPS'!

Don't forget to put their address at the top and date the letter. This letter uses the same basic strategy as the leaflet; it mentions their problem, indicates that things could become worse and then offers a potential lifeline, but this lifeline isn't a specific offer of help. They have to call you to find out more, and their curiosity will usually compel them to do so.

A 'PS' is very effective in getting a point across

This is a very effective letter, written in plain, easy-to-understand English and does not sound like a circular. Take my tip and hand write each one, don't write one and photocopy the rest – it ruins the whole effect.

3. Newspaper advertising

There is no denying that newspaper advertisements work. However, a lot of thought needs to go into the copy, and to be effective the ads need to run continuously; the odd advertisement here and there is no good.

With newspaper advertising (and with all other types of media), the key is to be consistent – you need to instil familiarity and trust as people won't buy from you until they trust you. Trust and confidence take time to build up. To be successful with newspaper advertising you need persistence, patience, and a budget to keep the advertising running long enough to build that trust.

Your ad should appear in the same place in the newspaper at least weekly for an indefinite period (forever). Expect to run your newspaper advertising for two months before you see an increase in uptake. It takes some time to build trust, and if you quit, you'll have to start all over again. Don't waste your money starting a newspaper advertising programme if you don't have the time or funds to make it work.

Continuously running adverts, however, can be very expensive. What's more, to be *really* effective, you should consider more than one newspaper, and have differently written copy in each one. By running different ads you can gauge the effectiveness of each one. If one

> **To be effective, newspaper ads need to run continuously**

particular ad does not produce inquiries, or very few, then it obviously does not work and should be changed.

Professional copywriters keep what is known as a 'swipe file'. This is a folder of memorable headlines and advertising copy they come across, and is useful for inspiration. After all, if you find it memorable, the rest of the public probably will too! Buy a scrapbook and cut out memorable headlines or copy that you think might be helpful to you.

Remember that the longer you book your ad for, the cheaper it will be, and you should always negotiate the price. Regardless of what the advertising department may tell you, there is always room for manoeuvre and the closer it gets to publication date, the more leverage you have in negotiating the price.

Design tips

Here are some general design ideas for newspaper advertising.

1. Your newspaper advertising has a zero percent chance of succeeding if your prospect doesn't notice it. Attention is everything in newspaper advertising. You need visual impact (photos), white space, a distinctive border, a readable font, an eye-catching colour or whatever else it takes to stand out on the page. You newspaper advertising must be distinctive, unusual, and it should contrast with the other ads on the page. Be different.

2. Paste your draft ad into the newspaper to get an idea of whether or not it will stand out.

3. Where your ad is placed really matters. If your quarter-page ad falls against the fold of the paper, your readership will be cut by half. Poor placement could cost you one half of your customers. Buy a different shaped ad that will guarantee you an outside placement. What is the paper offering? Run of press (ROP) positioning means that the publisher is free to place your ad anywhere in the normal pages of the paper. This could be catastrophic: your ad may never be read.

With a preferred position, your ad goes in a specific section, or near the top of a page that has reading matter on it. A near reading (NR) position is placement anywhere on a page near reading matter. This is better, because people reading the paper spend more time on that page. You want your ad to be on a page where people spend time reading. The longer they stay on the

You should always negotiate the price

page with your ad the better. You will normally pay a premium of 10%–50% for good position, but it's probably worth it. Good positioning could double or triple your response rate.

4. Use only serif typeface for copy. It boosts reading speed, and can increase comprehension by up to 300% over other fonts.

5. Editorial style advertising increases readership by over 50%. With editorial style advertising, the copy is laid out like a regular news story. The word 'advertisement' always appears above the copy. If you have a story to tell, think about using editorial style advertising.

6. Your newspaper advertising should be easy to look at and easy to read. Bad sentence structure will reduce comprehension.

7. Use 12 point type for copy. Use 14 point type if your customers are senior citizens.

8. Don't use technical jargon. You will lose too many readers.

9. Make sure photos face into your ad, not outwards or towards a competitor's ad.

10. Make sure your newspaper advertising looks different from your competitor's. Don't advertise for them.

11. Vary sentence and paragraph length. Eight words per sentence will get the highest readership.

12. A smaller ad should have a single focus – one solution for one problem.

13. Busy layouts can often work better than clean, balanced ads because they keep the reader involved.

14. Use benefit captions under your photos in all of your newspaper advertising. These will get read.

15. Word your offer carefully and clearly. Your offer is a promise about the level of service you will deliver to your customers. Your offer will set your customers expectations, so you want to be very clear.

16. Discount coupons get the highest response rate for all printed marketing materials. Use one if you can in your newspaper advertising.

Newspaper advertising strategy depends on the type of business involved. The key question is, 'When and where (in which newspaper sections on which days) do your customers look for your type of business?'

General placement guidelines

1. A smaller advertisement run repeatedly will do better than a larger ad run less often. Remember: familiarity = trust. People respond to adverts they trust.

2. Shoppers read the Friday, Saturday and Sunday papers to plan their weekend shopping. Saturday is the most important of the three, but Sunday is the most widely read. If you are a retail store, you probably want your newspaper advertising to run on these days.

3. The public knows to read the paper on certain days of the week to get certain information. If your competitors are all running their newspaper advertising on Wednesday in the same section, there is a reason. Shoppers know to look there for information about your type of business.

If you change your ad and your customers don't recognize it, you will have wasted all of the trust you have built up over time. Many companies never change their basic newspaper advertising design. This is a good strategy as long as the ads are working.

You will see us repeat this idea over and over. Your ad has a zero percent chance of succeeding if your prospect doesn't read it.

Attention is everything in newspaper advertising. Don't be shy. You want the biggest ad that makes economic sense,

Where your ad is placed really matters

and the most stunning presentation you can design. Your ad must stand out from (and contrast with) all of the others on the page. Conservative ads won't even get noticed. Think about it.

Direct response newspaper advertising

Once you get their attention, your newspaper advertising needs to

Your ad has a zero percent chance of succeeding if your prospect doesn't read it

motivate your prospects to respond *now*. A direct response ad is written to get attention, interest, desire, and action immediately. Think of it this way: where will that newspaper be in 24 hours? In the recycling bin. Now, think about that huge mountain

of inertia you must overcome with your customers to get action. How are you going to get them to respond?

The best way is to use direct response newspaper advertising, and create professional advertisements using professional marketing techniques. You need to build real motivation in your customers if you want them to respond to your newspaper advertising.

More direct response newspaper advertising

Let's see if we can help you to better recognize effective direct response advertising. Here's an example;

Hungry?
Try Our 99p Double Cheeseburger

This ad achieves one-to-one communication, and motivates the reader to recognize a problem (hunger) by asking a stimulating question. 'Hungry?' asks the ad. 'Yes', the reader replies, 'That's me.' The ad then offers an immediate, highly desirable solution.

'Try Our 99p Double Cheeseburger' (problem, solution, value, desire, satisfaction).

The ad gets visual attention simply by using special fonts. It gets attention, identifies a problem (stimulates interest), creates desire, and demands immediate action. Notice that this newspaper advertising does not *ask* the reader to try the product – it *tells* him to try it. If the reader is hungry this ad can stimulate a physical reaction in his stomach and in his mouth. Using the right colours in the ad will increase this physical reaction. A full colour photo of the product could make your stomach grumble. Get the idea?

Advertising needs to motivate your prospects to respond now

This deceptively simple newspaper advertising works. It is written to get a response, and it does.

A direct response advertisement:

1. Gets attention through design, ad size, placement, and timing;

2. Stimulates interest by touching on human emotions, desires, and needs;

3. Creates desire by offering solutions (benefits) to emotions, problems, or needs;

4. Gets action by making the solution highly desirable yet affordable and easy.

This is professional newspaper advertising. Use it.

4. Internet advertising

This subject is so huge today it is impossible to cover it all in this book, so we will just go over the basics.

A website is a collection of advertising pages, nothing more. The difference is that you can show a lot more information than in, say, a newspaper ad or a leaflet, and receive an instant response.

However, it doesn't matter how good your website is if no one reads it! A website must be seen, and to be seen it needs to appear on the first couple of pages on a search engine (Google being the most obvious example) There are ways of achieving this using key words, meta tags and pay-per-click, and this process is known as search engine optimization, or SEO. If you don't know how to do this yourself, pay someone else to do it for you; it is essential.

A website is a collection of advertising pages

Your web pages need to be written with the foregoing rules on copywriting in mind. You still need to grab your prospect's attention quickly, and you need to hold on to it long enough to get him to the point where he fills in his details.

The more information you can grab, the more valuable the contact. The basics are just a name and email address, but you can go all the way to phone numbers, gender, age, home address, occupation, what the reader is looking for, and anything else you may consider relevant to your business. Bear in mind though that asking for too much information and making the application laborious might just put some people off completing the form.

Give thought to the domain name you give your website. You could use your name; for example, www.johnsmith.co.uk, but the likelihood of anyone coming across your site is remote, to say the least. Think of the keywords your prospects will type into a search engine. They are likely to type 'stop repossession', 'money problems', 'can't pay the mortgage', 'sell my house fast' or anything else relevant to their

The more information you can grab, the more valuable the contact

problem. They won't type in 'John Smith'! Note also that they will use the first person when typing; 'Sell *my* house fast'. You will get more response if you entitle your website similarly; use 'my', and not 'your'. No one will type into Google 'Sell *your* house fast'.

5. Other lead sources

There are lots of other property investors out there who are advertising for business. Often they are after the 25% below market value leads. Their strategy is to buy below market value – the lower the better – to then either refurb, flip or add to their portfolio.

Now it stands to reason that not all calls they receive will be from sellers who have 25%, 20%, or any equity in their property. What, then, do the investors do with these leads? Often, they dump them. They don't do anything with them!

This is fantastic, because here is a rich source of leads. Of course, nothing is free, so when you call them to ask if they would be so kind as to pass their unwanted leads to you, you'll offer them a cash incentive for every lead converted to a deal. The amount is up to you, but between £250 and £500 is generally considered acceptable.

Where do you find these investors? They mostly advertise by leaflets, in newspapers, and quite often the local free papers. Pick these papers up whenever you see them, and look out for ads saying, 'Sell your house fast' or similar, and give them a call.

6. Estate agents

I get almost all my leads from estate agents. Whenever I say that, I get raised eyebrows, and I can understand why. Estate agents are not the easiest people to negotiate with! However, when you look at things from their perspective it is not difficult to see why. Estate agents are trained to think and negotiate in a certain way, and they often have difficulty thinking 'outside the box'.

I get almost all my leads from estate agents

Still, once you have converted them to your way of thinking, they are enthusiastic sources of leads and, ultimately, deals.

The secret is in the way you approach them. Walking in off the street and coming across as the great 'I Am', will get you absolutely nowhere. They have seen it all before, many times, and the cloak of scepticism fits them very well. Anyway, they have their favourite investors, and the deals go to them; they are tried and trusted. Why should they risk the status quo by dealing with an unknown?

They don't know, of course, that you have a different tactic to negotiate. They naturally think you are after BMV deals, like everyone else.

There *is* a way to work with estate agents, and I use it with great success. It does require persistence but your effort will be well rewarded.

So how can estate agents help us with lease option deals? Well, where, ninety-nine times out of a hundred, do people go when they want to sell their house? Yes, estate agents. The agents will generally be quick at determining the marketability and saleability of a property. They will, of course, tell a prospective vendor that the house will fetch more than they know it will in order to secure the commission, knowing that they will have to mark the property down later when it doesn't sell at the higher price.

In this game, visibility is credibility

There is always the problem property though; the one that won't sell because there is not enough equity in there to reduce the price to secure a sale. They are 'sticky', unsellable properties. Estate agents don't like them because they know they will be sitting on their books and taking up space in their window, they won't sell, they don't earn commission and they have angry vendors on the phone every other day demanding answers.

The trouble is, they have to take them on, because if they don't, their competitors will. In this game, visibility is credibility, and it is important for the agents to have the maximum number of 'For Sale' boards up, to the detriment of their competitors.

Your task is to convince the agents that these problematic, unsellable, non-fee-paying properties can in fact generate a considerable amount of income for them. And for you. We will cover negotiating with estate agents more fully in the next chapter.

5

Negotiation

There are many, many books written on negotiation and sales technique and I recommend very highly that you buy or borrow some and learn all you can about this fascinating subject if you want to have even a small chance of success in any field, not just property.

Selling is simply persuasion. Persuading someone to your point of view, whether that view is that a particular item is one they want to buy, that they should take a particular course of action, or that they will find us attractive. What we are doing is *marketing*, or *selling*. We sell ourselves constantly, in the way we dress, behave, interact with people ... and we are sold to constantly. We can't open a newspaper or switch on the TV without being subjected to a barrage of advertising. It's not just direct advertising either. We are constantly being manoeuvered into a way of life by TV programmes and the media: we must be slim, fit, tolerant, busy, have such and such a car, and dress and

Selling is simply persuasion

feed our children in such a way. A lot of it is subtle, but no less effective for that.

Negotiation, therefore, is selling. First we have to sell ourselves. People, generally, buy from people they like, and people generally like people who are similar to themselves. We have to persuade the other person to like us.

Imagine going to the bank for a loan. If you have never met, and don't know the manager, to him you are just an account number and a transaction history. Bank managers are very straight people: they follow the rules. They wear suits to work, think and act in a particular way and, what is more, you expect them to do so.

So go to see him wearing dirty trainers, a hooded jacket and tee-shirt, and what reaction would you expect to receive? What would his likely view of you be? Do you think he is going to say to himself, 'Now here is a good, hardworking, decent, upright citizen worth lending money to?' Or is he more likely to group you with the feral people who riot and cause mayhem

People generally buy from people they like

in our society? Right or wrong, he is going to make a decision. You could help yourself by having a haircut, dressing in a suit and cleaning your shoes. In other words, trying to be more like him.

The dress code is only a part of it, however. Your demeanor is also very important. Think about the sort of people you might be attracted to. Smiling, happy, bright, conversational, friendly or surly, rude, aggressive and monosyllabic? Of course people like friendly people. We gravitate towards them. That is because happy, friendly people make us feel good.

Not only that, but people naturally want to associate with successful people. Bank managers are no exception. They are people, after all, Not only that, but bank managers often have a great respect for entrepreneurs, especially successful ones, because such people are not what bank managers are made of.

Bank managers are chosen for their safety. The last thing a bank needs is a manager with an entrepreneurial bent. They want one who is stable, safe and follows the rules.

I remember, years ago, reading Aristotle Onnassis' book. He was once asked the question; 'Aristotle, what advice would you give to a budding entrepreneur?' His answer? 'Always wear the best suit you can afford and always have a suntan'. The reason, of course, is that it gives an image of success, and people like

Always wear the best suit you can afford

to associate with successful people in the hope that some of that success will rub off.

Therefore, dress to impress, be smiling, happy and friendly, and you're halfway there.

There are two main parts to a sales pitch. The first is to sell the *concept*. The second is to negotiate the *terms*. It is absolutely pointless moving on to the terms of a deal if the other party is not completely convinced of the concept of what you are trying to sell.

So how do we know whether the other party is happy with the concept or not? Simple. Ask them. Many junior or new salesman are afraid of asking direct questions in case they receive a negative answer. In fact, the whole point of a direct question is to determine whether the other party has a problem with what

Everybody has a hot button

you are trying to sell. If they have, you need to find out *now*, and address the problem to their satisfaction before you can move on to the next part. If you don't, those problems will surface at the end in the form of 'I'll think about it', or 'I have to speak to my wife/ mum/uncle' or 'my dog just died' or any other daft excuse that the majority of salesmen are so used to.

As you go through your presentation you should use *test closes* to make sure that any objections the other party may have are brought out into the open and dealt with. A close is confirmation from the prospect of a deal. Test closes are periodic, mini closes to ascertain whether the prospect is happy with the way the negotiation is proceeding.

Everybody you negotiate with will have a motivating factor, a *hot button* that is the key to unlocking their natural reticence and securing a deal. Discovering that hot button is absolutely key in bringing the negotiation to a swift and favourable close. So how do we find out what the other party's hot button is? Simple. Ask them.

Ask right out. Just say; 'Mr and Mrs Smith, I understand that you have a problem and need to sell your house fast. Could you tell me what your problem is and what you would consider an acceptable solution?'

You will probably be very surprised at the answers you receive. Typical answers are; 'We are divorcing and just need to get rid of the house quickly'. I have lost my job and can't afford the mortgage. I just want out quickly'. 'I just want to walk away without having to pay the mortgage'.

It is like manna from heaven. You now know exactly what they need, and you know how to proceed with your sales pitch to give them exactly what they want.

Remember though, what people *say* and what people *mean* are often two different things. In negotiation people will start with an optimistic goal, and can usually be negotiated down. Remember too, that there are no rules in negotiation, and not being wholly truthful is completely acceptable. For example, if you are negotiating with an estate agent, and you tell him that you absolutely must have a particular property, you put yourself in a very weak position indeed. Better by far to say that whilst you

Negotiation is a system of compromise

would like it, you have other properties you are negotiating at the moment, so you're not desperate.

It's a funny thing, but have you noticed that when you are negotiating with an agent and discussing an offer, there is always another potential buyer who has made an offer, and that you really need to raise yours if you want the property! It's not untruths really, it's gamesmanship. OK, it's untruths ... but it happens.

We tend to think of negotiation as just talking, listening and bargaining, but it can take many other non-verbal forms too. For instance, cancelling a planned meeting, cutting short a phone call, taking an 'important' call during a meeting, are all negotiation techniques designed to put pressure on the other party.

Negotiation is a system of compromise. We rarely get exactly what we want in a deal, and we generally settle for something less, but still acceptable. Imagine buying a car. Unless you are a complete novice, you will always try to negotiate a better deal. Say the asking price is £5250. You reckon you can get it for £5000, so you offer £4750. The salesman tuts and says he can't do that. You expected that, so you up your offer to £4900. The salesman says he just has to go and check with the manager (this technique is called reverting to a higher authority – you can't argue with someone who isn't there and supposedly has the final

A deal needs to be good for both sides

word). The salesman comes back and says that the manager, (after the salesman had negotiated hard on your behalf) has agreed that you can have it for £5000. You are delighted, because you got your deal, right?

Wrong. You just got screwed. In fact you paid exactly the price the garage wanted, and because you were not proficient in negotiation techniques and tactics, you didn't see them being used against you, and you didn't even establish the correct price in the first place.

Still, you went away happy, and the salesman was happy too, so that made a good deal. A deal needs to be good for both sides to be a good deal.

Imagine if you had gone to that garage and offered £5000 straight out. The salesman immediately says 'Yes', because he has his target price. You pay your money and drive off. However, before long doubt starts to creep in. The salesman didn't negotiate, he just said 'yes' straight

In negotiation, not being wholly truthful is completely acceptable

away. It was just too easy. Maybe you should have gone lower, maybe you could have got a better price. It starts to niggle, and the deal no longer looks so good.

The salesman goes and tells his manager what a good sale he just made. The manager looks at him and asks why he didn't negotiate for a higher price. He just accepted the customer's first offer;

almost certainly he could have done a better deal. Suddenly the salesman isn't so happy with the deal either.

Result? Neither party is happy that they got the best deal they could, and in circumstances where the customer can cancel, he now will. It's called 'buyer's remorse'.

The one thing that absolutely everyone wants from a negotiation is a feeling of satisfaction, and, to be successful, you need to negotiate in such a way that the other party feels that satisfaction. Screwing someone to the wall and ripping their guts out because they are vulnerable and you can, will only rebound on you in some way. I illustrate this point on my courses with a true story.

In the mid-eighties my wife and I booked a holiday in Turkey, and a friend of my wife, Sandra, came along. Sandra's aim on the holiday was to buy an oval lace tablecloth. She knew exactly what she wanted, and she knew from friends that she could buy one in Turkey much cheaper than back in the UK.

While browsing the books in duty free I came across one called *Everything is Negotiable*, by Gavin Kennedy, and bought it. It wasn't a very long book, and I read it through on the plane. However, it opened my eyes to a whole new world of negotiation.

There were plenty of locals selling produce on the beach, and eventually an old lady – who looked about 130 years old – came over to us with an assortment of lacework. Our friend Sandra looked through and found exactly what she wanted. She asked how much, and Old Lady told her it was £130, or the equivalent in Turkish Liras. Sandra bargained hard, and a deal was struck at £100. Delighted, she went off to change some money, but I decided that I would use the techniques I had just read in the book to see if I could get the price lower, and started negotiating. I was still negotiating when Sandra came back with the money, and finally, two hours later, Old Lady grudgingly accepted my price.

£4!!!

Yes, you read that correctly. **Four pounds!**

Mind you, Old Lady hated me. She threw the tablecloth over, spat, cursed, cried and kicked sand at us. Sandra paid the £4 but the deal was spoiled because she felt sorry for Old Lady. My day was spoiled too, because Sandra and my wife thought I was a mean git and a right b*****d. In retrospect, both

> **You need to establish who has the authority**

parties would have been absolutely delighted with a sale at £50 and I would not have got the silent treatment.

I don't tell this story to brag about my negotiating prowess, but to show that both sides do, really, have to be satisfied for the deal to be good.

Negotiation is not all about one side winning everything and the other side losing all. You can certainly be aggressive and intimidating, and you may get more than you thought you could. You can also get rich robbing banks if you don't get caught, but do you really want to live that way? Do you really want a reputation that is so bad that nobody wants to deal with you?

You will have more success and do more deals if you are a nice person to do business with. That does not mean being weak. You can – must – be firm and use all tactics available to you, but it takes less energy and emotional strain to be pleasant and it is much better to have people like you than hate you.

Estate agents

As mentioned earlier, negotiating with estate agents is likely to be the hardest part of your job. Not because they are fantastic negotiators necessarily, although they do have training in sales and negotiation techniques, but because they often have a blinkered view on property sales.

In an estate agent's world there is only one way for a property deal to proceed. They take an instruction, advertise and take

You need to be a chameleon

prospective buyers on a viewing. The agent negotiates the highest price they can possibly get (because their commission is percentage-based) takes the buyer's deposit, refers him to their mortgage advisor, arranges a survey, etc. (see chapter 2).

Asking them to think outside that particular box can sometimes be an uphill struggle, but when you succeed, you often have a rich source of leads and potential deals.

In any office there is one person who has the authority to consider creative deals, and that is usually the manager. Sometimes, though, the manager cannot deviate from his company guidelines, and that is often the case with large organisations. You need to establish who in the organisation has the authority to make creative decisions and contact him or her.

It pays when you are negotiating to know all you can about the other person. You need to be a chameleon and adapt your persona to match theirs. For instance, if you find that your contact is 'one of the boys', likes a pint after work and tells ribald jokes, it might be a good idea to invite him for a drink when his day is finished. On the other hand, if you need to negotiate with a family man with strict morals, telling saucy jokes is hardly going to get you any deals!

One way to find out such information is to register with an estate agent and book a couple of viewings, during which you can make friends with the person showing you round and ask him about how his office works, is he happy there, what the manager is like etc. Obviously you do this in a subtle way! No need to behave like a quiz master.

Armed with this info, you can now call the office and ask to speak with the manager. You adapt your speech to mirror his personality – businesslike, friendly, jokey, etc. It is better to call first rather than wander in off the street. It shows professionalism and you will get to meet the manager when you know he has time to devote to you.

The only purpose of the call is to set up a face-to-face meeting. Nothing else. Granted, in order to achieve that, you will have to give him some information, but be very careful about what and how much information you give him. Don't, under any circumstances, mention the words

It is better to call first than to wander in off the street

'lease option'. You will just frighten him away. If you give him too much information he will make a decision there and then and his answer will usually be that he is too busy.

A successful call might go like this:

You: *Oh, hello Mr Smith, sorry to disturb you when you're busy, but I wonder if I might make an appointment to come and see you in the office.*

Mr S.: *Well, what do you want to see me about?*

You: *I've got an idea that I think will interest you, and that could make us both a substantial amount of money, and I'd like to talk to you about it.*

Mr S.: *What is it?*

You: *Well, it's a bit involved to go into over the phone, and besides, I have some paperwork to show you so I thought if you could give me five minutes...*

Mr S.: *Erm, ok, how about this afternoon?*

This is a typical phone conversation that gets you through the door, after which you will, hopefully, have his undivided attention.

The paperwork you mentioned, and that you will take with you, explains everything that the manager needs to know; a mini business plan, in effect (I provide all this paperwork on my courses). Most important, it tells him how much money he can make out of 'unsellable' properties. You give him that as a back-up, because you can bet that fifteen minutes after you have left the office

Be sure to wear the 'uniform'

he will have forgotten what you said. Having that paperwork in front of him will act as a reminder, assuming he doesn't just chuck it in the bin.

The idea is that you nail him down to an agreement at that meeting, and so you should go prepared with everything you need to achieve that. Be sure to wear the 'uniform'. Estate agents wear suits, and you will look more professional if you do too, rather than jeans and trainers. You're in business, so wear business attire.

Remember that this meeting is your sales pitch. You are going to sell yourself and your business idea. Whilst the manager is likely to be friendly, be aware that he sees a great many people like you, and he is more than likely feeling pretty sceptical. Knowing this, plus any information you managed to pick up about him puts you one step ahead.

Say, for instance, that you have discovered that he is a keen golfer. An opening line might be:

'Hello Mr Smith, thanks for seeing me, although I know I'd rather be out on the links right now!' (Assuming the weather isn't inclement)

Straight away that breaks the ice, and gives a mutual point of contact. Beware, though, of coming across as an expert golfer if

Test close periodically

you're not. He will suss you out very quickly and you will have shot your credibility to pieces. Much better to come across as a novice, rather than an expert, even if you are an expert. Ask his advice about your swing if the conversation moves into golf – it will make him feel good.

Having established a rapport, gently move into your sales pitch, but don't let it look like a sales pitch. The principles are the same though.

Identify his pain – in this case, unsellable properties – and all the problems they cause. Offer a solution – lease options – and what is in it for him. Close him. Sounds simple, and it is really, when done right. The trouble is, it is easy to get sidetracked: a dominant opponent will soon control the meeting and you are lost.

So what is his pain? It's the unsellable properties he has on his books; the ones with little, no or even negative equity. The agents, who gave the vendor an optimistic price in order to secure the instruction, know that it is impossible to lower the price enough in today's market to secure a sale, and the house is going to sit there on their books, gathering dust. The vendor will give them constant grief, and the negative impact of having a 'For Sale' sign outside a property for too long almost cancels out the problem of having a competitor's board there.

Once the manager realises that you know about these properties and can offer a solution to the problem, he is likely to be all ears. Remember to test close periodically:

'So, Mr Smith, if I could give you a solution that means you can get these properties off your books and make you a considerable amount of money, would you be interested?'

Once you have explained a point, ask him if he is OK with that. This is crucial. If he has a problem with anything you need to know *now* and sort it out before you go any further otherwise it will crop up later and spoil the deal.

So what can you offer him? You could offer, say, £10 for every lead you receive, and £150 for every deal you close. You could then let the agency manage the property for you for the length of the option (assuming they handle lettings as well as sales) and at the end, he will get his commission from the vendor, and a commission from you if you decide to flip at that point. Not a bad income from an unsellable property.

Don't forget that what you are offering are the terms of the deal. Don't move on to them until you have complete agreement with the concept of lease options. When you do have a deal, ask to make it exclusive: you don't want to share your hard-earned arrangement with anyone else.

Not all meetings will result in a deal, however: there are plenty of managers who can't see the deal. No matter. Don't get stroppy. You know it's going to happen, but these are early days. Explain that it is no problem; you have other agents to see and if he changes his mind, would he please contact you. Always leave the door open for further negotiation.

You can use his negativity now when you meet your next manger. During your opening chat you could say, 'Mr Jones, I've just been **Always** to see Mr Smith at Dullards Estate Agency, and **ask for an** would you believe that he just could not see the **exclusive deal** sense in what I am saying…'. The implication, of course is that Mr Jones would look just as daft were he unable to see the sense in what you are saying! He is likely to want to appear smarter than Mr Smith.

As soon as you have tied up a deal, and completed your first lease option, go back to Mr Smith at Dullards and say, 'Mr Smith, you might remember that I came to see you about some business a while ago and you decided it wasn't for you? Well, Mr Jones at Smart Estate Agency decided to give it a go, and we've just completed our first deal. Can I show you just how much money Mr Jones is going to make?'

You can now go through the deal, itemising and totalling the income over the option period, plus exit commission fees. If Mr Smith does not want to go along with you now, just contact his area manger, or whoever controls him. Regardless, with this deal in your pocket, you have proof that the system works whoever you talk with.

The vendors

Negotiating with vendors is a completely different matter. Often the vendors you meet are in a very vulnerable and stressful situation. They usually have financial problems, may be facing repossession, find little in the future to look forward to so the last thing they need is some 'suit' being over-bearing.

Treat the vendors as people, not numbers

Dress for the part, then. Smart but casual. They are likely to associate suits with the people who got them into the mess they are in; bankers, employers, the government (anybody but themselves, in fact) and those people wear suits.

The vendor needs to like and trust you, so spend some time getting to know him; stroking the cat, playing with the kids; anything that relaxes and produces an atmosphere more conducive to a friendly chat.

You need to show empathy with the vendor, be sympathetic to his problems. So ask him what the cause of his problem is. You

Nothing is impossible and everything is negotiable

may get answers such as 'the bank', 'the company I worked for', or 'the economy'. This other entity is seen as the 'baddie', and we are going to join forces to fight them. Once you know who the baddie is you can align yourself with the vendor by talking about 'us' against 'them' ('Don't worry Mr Green, I'm sure we can sort those banks out between us').

Don't be pushy with these vendors. They are usually not 'motivated sellers', but 'distressed sellers', and need understanding and hand-holding. They need to know their home is going to be looked after, and that they are being treated as people, not numbers. Remember that you are still in a sales process, and the usual rules apply. You need to identify their pain, and offer a solution.

The best way to get them to really understand their pain is to get them to tell you what it is:

You: *Tell me Mrs Green, what will happen if you can't find a solution to your problem?*

Mrs G.: *Well, the bank will repossess the house and we might be bankrupt.*

Now we can try a test close:

You: *So, if I could find a solution that could prevent all that, would you be interested?*

Mrs G.: *Ooh, yes!*

Let's emphasize the problem a little more:

You: *The problem, though, is that you can't find a buyer, is that right?*

Mrs G.: *Yes, the house has been on the market for nine months and we haven't even had a viewing...*

You: *Why do you think that is?*

Mrs G.: *Well, it's the economy, isn't it? The banks and everything...*

You: Yes, they've messed a lot of people's lives up, haven't they?

Mrs G.: Yes

Now we test close again:

You: *Mrs Green, if we could find a buyer this week and take the house and its problems off your hands, would you be happy with that?*

Mrs G.: *Ooh, yes!*

Now we can offer a solution:

You: *Well Mrs Green, the good news is that I am sure we can find you a buyer, but not just yet. We have to wait until the economy improves. However, what if we pay your mortgage for you until that happens?*

Mrs G.: *Oh, really?*

You: *Yes, we would pay your mortgage and council tax and make sure* *your home is fully maintained. You could move out into the flat you want, and we would take care of all your problems; no repossession, no bankruptcy. How does that sound?*

Mrs G.: *Ooh, wonderful!'*

Notice that there is absolutely no mention of the words 'lease option' or 'scheme'. Telling a vulnerable vendor that you have a 'scheme called a lease option' will get you absolutely nowhere.

You have just sold the concept. Now, after a cup of tea, you discuss the terms, and these would be the length of the option, the purchase price at the end and the basics of the contract. Produce a notepad and a pen, and have *them* write down **Do not use the words 'scheme' or 'lease option'** the heads of terms agreement (the terms you both agree on). There are two reasons for this. If they are writing and you propose something they are not sure about, or disagree with, they will stop writing, and you have the chance there and then to sort out the problem. Also, the fact that they have written it out and signed it will cement the deal in their mind.

Easy! Deal done!

However, not all deals are as quick and easy as that (although a lot are). Often there are problems that require a creative mind and strategy in order for the the deal to work.

6

Creative strategies

A lease option generally works very simply: you lease someone's property for an agreed time, paying the mortgage and ensuring their council tax liabilities are met and any maintenance is done, and at the end of that period you have an option to buy that property at the price agreed when the contract is drawn up. In the meantime you rent the property out and the difference between the mortgage and the rent is your profit.

However, not all deals are as straight forward as that. Often there are other factors which can complicate the proceedings, sometimes even to the point of making a deal unworkable: mortgage arrears and secured loans being the two main causes.

Mortgage arrears

Obviously, no one is facing the threat of repossession if the mortgage is paid up to date, but it goes without saying then that there will often be mortgage arrears in the current economic climate and it is here that your interest lies.

It is written into all residential mortgage agreements that the homeowner cannot let the property without permission from the mortgage company. This is not usually a problem. The mortgage companies cannot unreasonably withhold permission to let. Not surprisingly, arrears are seen as a reasonable excuse to refuse that permission.

Until that permission is granted, you cannot proceed with the deal, so you have no option but to pay off those arrears. However, to make your lease option contract legal, money needs to change hands (the *option price*). Usually this is a nominal £1, but in the above case the arrears you have paid are considered to be the option price.

Mortgage companies cannot unreasonably withhold permission to let

In your option agreement it should state that the option price is considered to be part of the *purchase price* – the price you pay for the property when you buy it – so you could consider the arrears payment as a loan to the property that you will recover when you exercise your option.

Do not be tempted to ignore the part about informing the mortgage company and having their permission. Not only is it illegal but it is seen as a default in the terms of the mortgage contract and the company is within its rights to then repossess the property.

Sometimes the homeowners just need some capital to move on. If they are struggling to pay their mortgage, they are unlikely to have enough spare cash lying around to afford the deposit for a rental property and the associated moving costs. You may need to pay them say, £1000 or so to move on. Again, this sum is considered to be the option price and you will recover it at the back end. Consider it an investment.

Secured loans

A bigger problem is a secured loan. During the middle of the last decade mortgages were easy to find, and the banks, awash with money, were offering loans to almost everyone. Many new homeowners took advantage of the easy loan to update their new home, refurbishing the kitchen and bathroom and decorating throughout.

The trouble is, that secured loan effectively put them into negative equity, and that is often the reason they cannot now sell their home. If anything is going to be a deal-breaker, it is a secured loan.

Incidentally, when you are performing your due diligence, you will of course ask the homeowner if they have any secured loans or other debts. Don't however, take

If anything is going to be a deal-breaker, it is a secured loan

their word for it if they say they haven't. Get a copy of the deeds from the Land Registry. If there are any secured loans, the banks details will be on the deeds as interested parties. It is amazing how many people 'forget' that they have a secured loan!

You now need to do your sums. Add together the outstanding mortgage and the secured loan to see how much the negative equity is. Negative equity in itself is **If the repossession went ahead the loan company would lose everything** not necessarily a problem. You can extend the *option period* (the time you lease the property from them for) to allow for the value of the property to rise above that figure.

A bigger problem with a secured loan is the monthly repayment figure, and whether or not the vendor can carry on paying it off after they move on. If they can, there is no problem as long as the mortgage payment/rental income figures stack up.

If they can't, you need to decide whether it is in your interest pay it off for them, and make adjustments, if you can, on the purchase price or whether it is just too much of a burden.

The problem is the fact that it is secured. Unsecured loans, such as credit cards or unsecured bank loans do not impact as much, although no loans at all, of course, are better from your point of view.

I completed a deal with one particular couple in the north east of England. I'll call them Jane and John, and I got their lead from an estate agent. Jane and John owned a two bed terraced house worth about £52,500. At the time their outstanding mortgage was £31,395, with monthly mortgage repayment of £222. Rental comparables were £400, so it was a reasonable deal. However, I discovered that they had a £50,000 secured loan, taken out when they bought the property. Who on earth though that it was a good idea to lend almost 100% of the value of the property that, at that time, had no equity, I have no idea. The loan company was not the mortgage provider, but a separate company.

The problem was that John had lost his job, and they needed to move into rented accommodation. Obviously, they could not sell. They had a house worth around £50,000 with equity of around £20,000, but with debts of over £80,000. On the face of it, it was not going to be a deal.

However, I didn't give up and asked them what would happen if they did not find some sort of acceptable solution. They would have to go the repossession route, they said, and default on the loan.

I looked at the figures again. Properties just were not selling at all in the North East, and the only hope the bank had would be to sell at auction, where they would be very lucky indeed to realise £35,000. After their costs, they would be losing a fair chunk of cash. More importantly, there would be absolutely nothing left for the loan company, who had second charge on the house. If the repossession went ahead the loan company would lose everything.

The only thing that John and Jane could do would be to contact the loan company and explain their situation – that they were about to be repossessed and that would mean defaulting on their loan, meaning the loan company would lose their money. The only chance John and Jane might have would be to do a lease option deal with me, but that was not possible with the loan secured on the property.

That would mean having the loan unsecured, but there was no security there now anyway, and at least John and Jane would continue to pay the loan instalments, so the loan company had a chance of getting their money back. It took some months, we had to give them all the paperwork and it was a boardroom decision, but the loan company agreed, and the deal went ahead.

When I mentioned what I was doing to other investors they all said 'They'll never go for that! It's impossible'. Nothing is impossible, and everything is negotiable.

Never put your own expectations onto other people. Just because *you* wouldn't do or agree to something doesn't mean that no one else would. You would be surprised at what people will do. Remember, if you don't ask, you don't get.

High mortgage payments

Another common problem is when the difference between the mortgage payment and the rental income is either too small or in a negative situation.

If there is no secured loan then the problem is often that the owners have tied themselves into a fixed repayment deal at a high interest rate. It is a simple procedure to find out to what rate the mortgage will revert and re-calculate on those figures.

Depending on when the fixed period ends you can either pay the difference yourself, accept a low cash flow or, preferably, ask the owner to pay the difference until the new rate comes into effect. Often, they will. Always keep in mind that you are a business, not a charity.

There is another solution, though, and that is to 'flip' the deal by acting as an agent.

For example, Mr Smith needs to sell his house quickly, and the outstanding mortgage is £100,000. Unfortunately, the current market value of the property is, at best, only about £95,000. In order to sell now, therefore, Mr. Smith will have to take a loss of £5000 on the price, the agent's fees, say, £1000, and possibly an early redemption fee to the mortgage company, say £2000. It could quite easily cost Mr Smith £8000 to sell his property now, even if he could find a buyer. Not a great situation. The problem for us is that the mortgage **Nothing is impossible and everything is negotiable** repayments are £500 per month, and the achievable rental income is also around £500 per month. Mr Smith is not able to contribute to the mortgage, so what can we do? Is the deal dead? No, not at all.

We advertise for a tenant buyer for the property at a price of £110,000. Mr Jones is interested and we agree a term of five years and monthly rental equal to the existing owner's mortgage. However, we ask Mr Jones for an up-front payment of £5000, with the final payment of £105,000 going to Mr Smith, out of which he will settle the mortgage, leaving him with a £5000 profit instead of a £8000 loss!

When Mr Jones exercises his option and buys the property, it will very likely be worth more than the £105,000 he is then paying, and he receives the benefit of the increased equity.

The £5000 that Mr Jones pays us is our fee for managing the deal, and must not be labelled a deposit at any time, otherwise you could lose it. Our profit is this £5000 fee – because of the mortgage level we cannot make an ongoing profit.

We structure the option agreement between Mr Smith and Mr Jones, and we can make ourselves the managers of the property, with a clause inserted that if, for any reason, Mr Jones decides not to go ahead with the deal, we can find a new tenant buyer and structure another deal.

7

Selling your options

Options are negotiable. That means that you can sell them! Options are bought and sold every day on the stock exchange, although you will, of course, sell yours privately.

You can sell the initial lead too, but whereas a qualified lead might just fetch £120 and an unqualified lead just £30, a fully completed lease option deal can fetch anything up to £6,000, depending on the financials, although an average figure would be closer to £3000. Still,

There are plenty of people willing to pay for completed deals

if you sell two out of every three deals you complete, you will make a fair amount of income and build a sizeable portfolio too.

There are plenty of people willing to pay for completed deals. It is easy to find enterprising people who will act as agents and sell your deals for you, for a commission. Just Google 'sell lease option deals' and you will find many.

In the lease option contract someone who buys your deal is known as the *assignee*, and you assign your contract to him or her.

8

The lease option contract

A lease option contract, although at first glance seeming complicated, is in fact a very simple document, in legal terms. It is just a formalized contract between you, the purchaser, and the other party, the owner.

However, the devil, as they say, is in the detail, and there are potential pitfalls if you try to write a contract yourself, or download one from the internet (they are usually American) and try to adapt it to your

The devil is in the detail

own requirements. You *must* use a properly written contract. You will eventually pay the price if you don't.

Be aware that not all solicitors, even conveyancing solicitors, know their way around a lease option contract. You should make sure that the solicitor you choose has experience of drawing up such documents.

The contract is actually in three parts; the lease option itself, a management contract, and a power of attorney contract.

The lease option contract is the main document whereby the owner agrees to lease the property (the property) to you for a stated period of time, (the option period) with you having the option (but not the obligation) to buy the property at any time within the option period for a price agreed at the time of making the contract (the purchase price).

It states the address and title number of the property, and the names and addresses of the owner and purchaser, the start and finish dates, the option price (the amount you paid for the option) and the purchase price.

As with all contracts it has pages of type defining any pertinent words in the contract, and explaining (at length) how to post a letter etc.!

There are places for all interested parties and their witness to sign. In law, and if no other arrangement had been made, all the rental income would belong to the owner of the property. We therefore have a management agreement in place that makes you, the purchaser, the manager for the owner, and your fee is the difference between the mortgage amount you must pay and the rental income. It also lists the obligations upon both the owner and purchaser regarding insurance, maintenance etc. It also has space for all the required signatures.

Some owners have been very difficult to find!

Your option period could be for as long as twenty years, and people drift apart and lose contact in that time. Also, it is not unknown that as the end of the option period approaches, some owners have been very difficult to find! In such a case it would be extremely difficult, if not impossible, to exercise your option and purchase the property.

The final part of the contract then is a power of attorney, whereby the owner gives you enduring, but limited, power of attorney to sign the sale papers on their behalf. It also allows you to pay the purchase price to yourself

The contract is not valid unless money has changed hands

(although it should be kept in a separate account for the owner).

The power of attorney allows you to converse with the mortgage company and any other interested party. What it does *not* do is allow you access to the owner's bank account! Again, there is space for all the required signatures.

Remember that the contract is not valid unless money has changed hands.

Assuming the lease option contracts are foolproof, and mine are, the only possible reasons the owners could contest the contract is on the grounds of unreasonableness (which I cover by offering them a percentage of the uplift in value) or by their asserting that they did not understand the contract, and did not know what they were signing.

Whilst I always recommend the owners take legal advice, some don't, being happy to read the contract through and just sign. I therefore have them sign a disclaimer, that states that:

a) I have recommended very highly that they seek legal advice.

b) If they choose not to seek legal advice they cannot hold me or any assignees responsible for any loss as a result.

c) They are not taking any drugs, whether prescribed or not, that might impair their judgement.

d) I have neither offered nor given any financial advice.

That covers pretty well any reason the owners could possibly use to contest the contract. It also covers me if the FSA, in their wisdom, might at any point look through my business dealing to see if I have ever given financial advice of the type that would require a licence issued by the FSA.

You cannot be too careful. It's always better to look ahead and anticipate potential problems, rather than have them sneak up on you whilst you are unprepared.

9

Sandwich options

No, a sandwich option is not a choice between tuna and cheese!

It is a way of maximizing your income and minimizing your risks on a lease option deal, and it works like this as detailed below.

Once you have secured your deal you need to find a tenant. Tenants are the worst part of being in property. A bad tenant can cost you thousands, a good one is a joy to have. The trouble is that to begin with you have no idea at which of those extremes your prospective tenant is. **Appearances can be deceptive** Appearances can be deceptive, too. I have had seemingly respectable people turn out to be a nightmare, and young, yobbish-looking people turn out to be model tenants.

Your ideal tenant would be someone who will look after the house as if it were their own, while they rent it from you. They are called tenant buyers.

The idea here is to find a tenant buyer; someone who cannot buy at present for some reason – bad credit, no deposit etc – and make a lease option deal with them, this time with you as the vendor and them as the purchaser.

You can make the purchase price high enough to give you your outgoing profit, and make the option period three months or so shorter than your period with your vendor. That will give you time to find a new buyer or extend your option period if the tenant buyer decides not to go ahead with the purchase.

You can ask the tenant for a 'consideration' for moving in (not a deposit: a deposit has to be protected and you can't spend it) of say 3% of the value of the property. You can also ask for a premium to the market rent of maybe £25 or £50 per month too.

As a further bonus, you can require that the tenant is liable for all maintenance, but if you do that you need to make sure you are thorough with your periodic checks to ensure the property really is being maintained. This *should* provide you with a secure tenant who will look after the property, minimizing voids

You can ask for a 'consideration' for moving in

and maintenance issues. You shouldn't need the services of a managing agent, either.

For the tenant buyers, the deal means peace of mind that the tenancy is secure (subject to the contract terms), and that they have a house they really can call home, to the point where you will allow them to improve the property (subject to your permission and good building practice). It is an ideal situation.

Finding a tenant buyer

Finding a tenant buyer is not as straight forward as finding an ordinary tenant, but not difficult, either.

The first thing to do is erect a sign outside the property saying something like:

Rent-to-Buy
Move in for just £3000
No mortgage required
Call 12345 456 456

Place an ad in your local paper along the same lines as the sign (but with property details and photo) and advertise on Rightmove and Gumtree.

When prospective tenants call, you must remember not too give too much detail over the phone. When they ask what it is all about (and they will) say, 'Well, why don't I just meet you at the property and we can go over it then'. Once they are inside the property it is much easier to sell it. The wife will be mentally sorting out the kitchen and the kids will be fighting over who has which bedroom.

You can explain to them the benefits of living in a house that they really can call home. If their credit rating is bad, the option period gives them time to repair their credit and save for a deposit. They now have something to look forward to as a family.

10

The future

We have already established that now is the right time to be getting into lease options because of the economic situation, but what of the future? What happens when the economy improves and there is more money around? Will we still be able to find suitable vendors?

Absolutely.

There will always be people who mismanage their finances. There will always be job losses and divorces. There will always be deaths and people needing to move quickly for all sorts of reasons. An improving economy also means higher interest rates. There will always be people who cannot afford those higher rates. Fear not. Candidates for lease options provide a rich feeding ground, and always will.

As the economy improves the housing market will also improve, and once again we will see prices rising quickly. What that means for us is a shorter option period with quicker turnover of properties and higher profits.

Following the FSA's regulation of the sale-and-rent-back situation questions are being asked about whether they will do the same with lease options.

I'm not sure how they could do that. Sale-and-rent-back involved the sale of a property, and the problem was that agents were giving financial advice to the vendors, which was the nail in the coffin.

Lease options are contracts, and it is hard to see how the FSA, or anyone else, could ban contracts! Let's face it, the whole world revolves around contracts. A simple agreement to do something or provide someone with something is a contract, and it would be a complete minefield if the FSA try to ban lease option contracts.

The only wedge they might have is the financial advice situation. That is why I make a point of not offering any financial advice whatsoever and having the vendors sign a disclaimer to that effect, and why I urge you to do the same.

Remember: don't take *any* chances in business.

11

Workflow sheet

When a lead is received:

- Get a quick idea of current valuation on Mouseprice.

- Use Rightmove to find rental comparables for the area.

- Establish the provisional maximum mortgage you can pay based on estimated rental.

- Use Google Earth and Streetview to look at the property and the area.

- Use Yell.com to find local letting agents and chat to them to find out about the area – schools, shops, public transport etc., and general demand for letting in the area. Check likely rentals.

- Call the vendor. Do this when you are composed and you are likely to catch the vendor at home (if you only have a mobile number). Always check that the vendor is free to talk.

- Introduce yourself and ask them what the problem is to see if you can HELP.

- Fill in as much of the lead sheet as you can (a lead sheet is simply a list of prepared questions you will ask the vendor). You don't have to go through it in order, asking a series of questions. Better to disguise the questions in general conversation.

- Recap with the vendors. Get them to tell you what their problems are and the likely outcome if they don't find a successful resolution.

- Tell them you'll have a chat with your partner and come back to them tomorrow. Don't, on this first call, give any idea of solutions etc. Be very non-committal.

- In the interim, consider your proposal, and download a copy of the deeds from Land Registry (costs £4.00). Check for any charges the vendor 'forgot' to mention.

- Call the vendor, and RECAP. You need to make sure they are fully aware of the PAIN this problem is causing.

- Ask them what outcome they would like. Often they just want to walk away without any problems.

- Offer your solution, avoiding the words 'lease option' and 'scheme'. For example, 'I'm sure we can find a buyer for your property, Mr Smith, but because of the equity problem and the general economy, it wouldn't be for a while yet. But what we can do is look after your home for you in the meantime, making sure the mortgage and council tax is paid and it is fully maintained; once the prices rise, we can sell it and you would then have a fairly substantial amount of cash coming to you. How does that sound?'

'Good. It means you can move on with your life without any worries or problems, knowing your property is in safe hands. That's what you'd like, isn't it?'

(Note; the use of the words 'home' and 'property' are selected for the specific emotional impact they have in those parts of the sentence. Don't change them.)

- Assuming that you now have full agreement on the concept, arrange a home visit to discuss the deal in detail. Make sure all interested parties are going to be there (difficult if it is a divorce situation).

- Print off two copies of the contracts at home.

- Meet with the vendors and establish their capacity to understand the contract. Explain that you like them to have independent legal advice so they can see that everything is completely legal and above board. Go through the terms of the contract in general, emphasizing the benefits to them. Make sure they are ABSOLUTELY happy with it.

- Tell them you can recommend a solicitor who often deals with your clients and understands the contract. Explain that there is a cost, but it is between £300 and £400 cheaper with your recommended solicitor. Establish whether they can afford it or not. If they can't, decide whether you want to pay the fee or not. If you do, it forms all or part of the option price, and as such comes off the purchase price at the back end.

- Explain where they sign, and the witness signatures, and that they should not date the contracts.

- Discuss a time frame.

- Take photographs and discuss what they will leave, etc.

- When they have signed the contracts, meet with them again and take *all* copies of the contracts. (You will need them to date them for the effective date, later)

- Ask them to call the mortgage company to give your name as renter.

- Ask for the insurance documents and everything they have relating to the mortgage, boiler certificates, guarantees for work done, etc.

- When you have everything you can agree a date for completion, sign the contracts and date them for the required day.

You now have the property! Start marketing.

12

What next?

If you are reading this, it is because you have bought the book. If you bought the book it is, presumably, because you are interested in investing in property.

Maybe you are a seasoned investor already, with a large portfolio built the traditional way, and you are now looking for new investment methods. It could be that you are a beginner, and don't know how to start investing. Whatever your current position, this book gives you all the information you need to begin, but I am fully aware that for many people, the only way they can learn is by personal teaching. If this applies to you, you may be interested in joining one of my one-day instructional courses.

The courses give you all that this book does, and more:

- In-depth discussions and examples;
- The opportunity to have your questions answered;
- Personal back-up afterwards to help you in your deals;
- Full instruction, help and back-up with the legal paperwork.

Our courses are generally held on the last weekend in the month (excluding August and December) and we regularly have course attendees completing deals by the following weekend. You can do that too. But only if you take action. I have a saying: *'If you don't do something, you end up doing nothing'.*

Think about it. The way you operate, think and perform has led you to the point where you are now. If you are hugely successful, that is good, you don't need me, but if you're not, you have to ask yourself some searching questions.

Are you happy not being successful? Are you happy not being rich? No? Then are you prepared to make an effort and change your methodology to become successful? You won't become successful doing what you have always done, or going into business half-heartedly. You don't have to be a genius to succeed, you don't have to have lots of money, but there are three things you do need: An idea, desire, and persistence.

I have given you the idea – lease options. More than that, I can give you the whole business model to work with. That gives you a head start. All you need to contribute is the desire and commitment/persistence. If you are willing to do that I will help you all I can.

So contact me now and book onto my course (The Art of Lease Options). It could easily be the best thing you ever did. Email me now at peter@trimoreinvestments.co.uk.

Please also visit my website: www.trimoreinvestments.co.uk for information on other courses and my personal mentoring programme.

Go on, do it now. You must take action: tomorrow you will have forgotton. Tomorrow you will be back in your old ways, on the road to nowhere.

If you really want to change your life, contact me now!

13

Useful websites

Leads – general

www.everytownandcity.com

www.propertysnake.co.uk

www.home.co.uk

www.globrix.com

Leads – auction sites

www.propertyauctionaction.co.uk

www.countrywidepropertyauctions.co.uk

www.repossessedhousesforsale.co.uk

www.mustbesold.com

Leads – chain-free property

www.propertyearth.net

www.whitehotproperty.co.uk

Property values

www.notlocation.com

www.upmystreet.com

www.zoopla.co.uk

www.mouseprice.com

www.ourproperty.co.uk

www.globrix.com

www.houseprices.co.uk

Property investors

www.quickmovenow.com

www.nationalpropertytrade.com

Letting

www.landlordreferencing.co.uk

Other

www.landreg.gov.uk

www.oft.gov.uk

www.avoidstampduty.com

www.theAdvisory.co.uk

Solicitors

www.alexanderlawyersllp.com – Mike and Dean Alexander.

www.ms-law.co.uk – Shimon Rudich.

www.bpe.co.uk – Richard Spencer.

www.sweeneymillersolicitors.co.uk – Peter Sweeney, Paul Miller.

And last but not least

www.trimoreinvestments.co.uk

www.monochromephotography.com

Appendix

For the sake of brevity, I have used the masculine – he – instead of continually and ponderously using he or she, his or hers, etc. Please be assured that my female readers are definitely in my thoughts.

Abbreviations

BTL – buy-to-let

BMV – below market value

DIC – decision in principle

FSA – Financial Services Authority

LTV – loan to value

NR – near reading

ROP – run of page

RICS – Royal Institute of Chartered Surveyors

SEO – search engine optimization

QE – quantative easing

About the author

Peter Hogan is a businessman and seasoned property investor. He bought his very first buy-to-let property in March, 1986, very soon followed by others.

A keen sportsman, he has represented Great Britain in two different sports. He is also a well-known and successful landscape photographer, and his own brand of photographic products sells throughout the world.

He spent most of his life in Jersey, Channel Islands, from where he travelled extensively, but has now made his home in Buckinghamshire.

Peter is a prolific investor, constantly seeking creative ways of investing. His love of teaching has led him to offer courses on all methods of property investment, and he also offers one-to-one coaching and mentoring. For more information and to contact him please visit his website www.trimoreinvestments.co.uk.